Then & Now
Cottingham

Then & Now
Cottingham

Rachel Waters

The History Press

Frontispiece: The Manor House is Cottingham's oldest inhabited building and is situated off the north-west side of Hallgate. It is thought to have been built in the late sixteenth century on the earthworks of Baynard Castle, a fortified medieval manor house. Local historian Dr David Neave describes it as 'one of the best surviving timber-framed farmhouses in the East Riding'. In the 1960s the house was in a state of disrepair, and was extensively and sympathetically restored, with a porch added in the style of the original building.

First published in 2007 by Tempus Publishing

Reprinted in 2009 by
The History Press
The Mill, Brimscombe Port,
Stroud, Gloucestershire. GL5 2QG
www.thehistorypress.co.uk

British Library Cataloguing in Publication Data.
A catalogue record for this book is available from the British Library.

ISBN 978 0 7524 4487 1

Typesetting and origination by
Tempus Publishing.
Printed and bound in England.

Contents

Acknowledgements

We are indebted to the Edwardian photographers and postcard producers, both the large national commercial companies like Messrs Frith, Scott and Lillywhite, and the smaller local postcard publishers, without whom this book would not have been possible.

The village of Cottingham had several small postcard producers, the most prolific being the brothers Herbert and Harold Tadman. This view, taken around 1908, of the east end of Hallgate is an example of their work, and would have been sold at the post office they ran on Hallgate.

Whilst most of the images used in this book are from my own collection, I must acknowledge Paul Gibson and Robert McMillan for their kind assistance in supplying a selection of the old images which complement my own throughout the book.

I would like to thank the members of the Cottingham Local History Society, including Geoff Bell and Peter McClure, for their help and support during the preparation of the text.

I would especially like to thank my friend and tutor Chris Ketchell, without whose encouragement during local history classes at the former Hull College Local History Unit I would not have produced research of my own.

This book is dedicated to the memory of Alison Judith Tunstall, 1971-1988.

Brief Bibliography

Allison, K.J. (Ed.); Oxford University Press; *The Victoria History of the Counties of England, A History of the County of East Yorkshire*, Volume IV; 1979.

Allison, K.J; East Yorkshire Local History Society; 'Hull Gent Seeks Country Residence' 1750-1850; 1981.

Allison, K.J; Cottingham Local History Society; *Cottingham Houses: A Complete List of Houses, with Dates of Building and Names of Architect, Builders and Owners*; 2001.

Green, Kenneth R.; Hutton Press; *Old Cottingham Remembered*; 1988.

Green, K.R. and Green, E.M; European Library; *Cottingham in Old Picture Postcards*; 1986.

Markham, John (Ed.); Highgate of Beverley; *Cottingham in the Twentieth Century, Researched, Written, and Compiled by Members of the Historic Cottingham Project*; 2005.

Pevsner, Nikolaus and Neave, David; Penguin Books; *Buildings of England, Yorkshire: York and the East Riding*; Second Edition, 1995.

Railton, Peter; Hutton Press; *Cottingham Schools in the Nineteenth Century, a Study of a Yorkshire Village Community*; 1986.

Waters, Rachel; Unpublished Notes; *A History of Brewing and Malting in Cottingham*; 2002.

Waters, Rachel; East Yorkshire Local History Society; *The East Yorkshire Historian*, Volume Six; 'Cottingham Postcard Publishers'; 2005.

Whitehouse, John; Cottingham Local History Society; *Mark Kirby and Cottingham Free School*; 1980.

Introduction

The village of Cottingham in the East Riding of Yorkshire derives its name from 'the homestead of Cotta's people'. It was mentioned in the Domesday Book of 1086, when it was described as being in the ownership of Hugh, son of Baudry, valued at £7, and having a population of 130. However, archaeological discoveries show that the area was inhabited for many years before the Norman Conquest; four gold bangles found in the 1860s were estimated to be over 2,000 years old.

In the year 1197 William de Stutville, lord of the manor, was granted a charter to hold a weekly market, and a licence to build a double-moated, palisaded manor house, later known as Baynard Castle.

By 1320 the then-lord, Thomas Wake, had been granted permission to build an Augustinian monastery in the village, later relocated and rebuilt as Haltemprice Priory to the south-west. The Wake family were also granted a licence to further fortify Baynard Castle, at the west end of Hallgate.

On Thomas' death the estate passed first to his sister Margaret, and then via her daughter Joan Plantagenet, 'the Fair Maid of Kent', to Thomas de Holand, Joan's husband. On De Holand's death Joan married her cousin Edward, 'the Black Prince'. The estate finally passed to Joan's first-born son, Sir Thomas de Holand, and the land was held by the de Holand family until the early 1400s, when the last male heir, Edmund de Holand, died.

Cottingham was then divided amongst Edmund's four surviving sisters. The four parts of the lordship became known as; Richmond, Sarum, Westmorland and Powis, named after the sisters' husbands. By the year 1500 the four manors had been reunited and passed into the ownership of the Crown, at which time Cottingham had a population of around 1,500.

By 1600 the parish of Cottingham extended from Eppleworth in the west to the River Hull in the east, north to Dunswell and south to the Spring Ditch (the present alignment of Prince's Avenue and Spring Bank) in Hull, an area of approximately 10,000 acres; this has given rise to the reputation that Cottingham is 'England's largest village', and whether or not this claim is true the original parish certainly covered a huge area.

In 1771 the common meadows, pastures, and some of the open fields farmed by the villagers were enclosed, the remaining open fields being enclosed in 1793. The Enclosure Acts saw villagers losing their rights to farm common land, which passed into the hands of private owners. Nationally it changed agriculture from a subsistence occupation to an industrial process. It was during the eighteenth century that Cottingham really thrived. In 1764 a branch of the Hull to Beverley turnpike was extended to Cottingham, providing access to the village via a safe and supposedly well-maintained road. As a result Cottingham became the country residence for many wealthy Hull business families, who were keen to escape the noise and smells of the overcrowded industrial town where they made their money. By the late eighteenth century many large Georgian merchant's houses had been built in the village, some of which survive. However the village was still predominantly agricultural, with most people employed in associated jobs.

In 1846 Cottingham was linked to the new railway network, when the Hull to Scarborough line opened, making the village even more accessible. Many members of the new middle classes were able to live in Cottingham and commute daily to their white-collar jobs in Hull. By 1850 the population was over 2,800 and demand for housing was high, with new residential streets being laid out all around the village. The new 'modern' developments around the railway station, built on agricultural land, were particularly popular. The 1911 census records the village's population as 4,648, with the building and population boom only halted by the outbreak of war in 1914.

Following the post-war depression Cottingham soon flourished again, and at the end of the 1920s the new University College of Hull opened, utilising some of the old Georgian merchant's houses as halls of residence for the influx of students into the village. When the college was granted university status in May 1954 student numbers increased to such an extent that even more old houses were purchased and converted into accommodation, thus saving them from almost certain demolition. Eventually a large purpose-built campus was developed to the north-west of the village, at the Lawns, to house students.

The 1920s also saw Cottingham's first development of 'social housing', with servicemen returning from the First World War being given first refusal. The inter-war years were possibly Cottingham's busiest in terms of house construction. By 1931 the population had risen to around 9,000, and demand for housing in the village continued. More agricultural land on the eastern and western peripheries of the village was developed, and many of the streets featured in this book bear testimony to the zeal of the 1930s builders. The outbreak of the Second World War saw all available materials and skilled men utilised for the war effort, effectively halting the village's development until peace was restored in 1945.

The war saw a change in the village's demographic; American and Free French troops occupied a camp on Harland Way (which later became the Lawns), and Dutch and Eastern European families settled in a displaced persons camp on Priory Road. Many of the latter settled locally and added much to village life.

Throughout the last sixty years Cottingham has continued to grow, initially due to post-war housing developments on both green field and so-called 'brown field' sites, where previously developed sites are reused. This type of building, with new housing being squeezed into every available space, has made up the majority of building in the village since the 1980s, and today Cottingham is the size of a small town, with a population of 17,800 recorded in the 2001 census. The village is now regarded as a fashionable commuter zone for the city of Kingston upon Hull, with excellent schools, health-care facilities and community organisations. However, it still manages to maintain its individuality; Hallgate and King Street retain a good selection of local shops, businesses and pubs, and a market is held on the historic Market Green every Thursday. Most recently the village has become famous for its ever more spectacular Christmas lights, which attract thousands of visitors for the switching-on ceremony in late November/early December.

This book tries to illustrate some of Cottingham's rich history through the development of its streets and buildings. Hopefully the photographs, both old and new, will refresh people's memories of what has gone, and help us appreciate and value that which survives. Some of the modern photographs show huge differences when compared to the older ones, whilst others show very subtle changes like television aerials, telephone wires, and UPVC windows. The biggest overall difference has to be the huge volume of traffic, which seems to dominate every modern photograph.

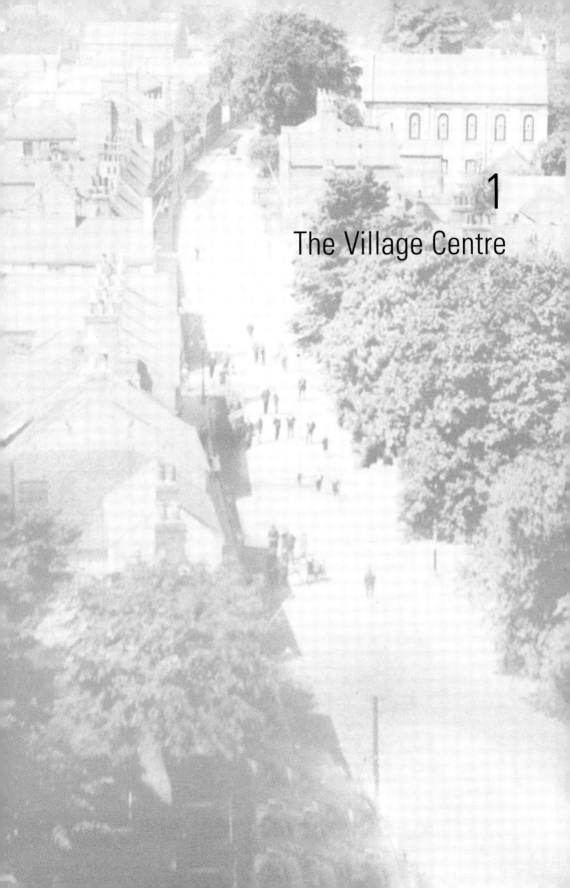

1

The Village Centre

*A*erial views are always popular and this photograph is from the Aerofilms series of postcards produced in the 1920s. These photos were taken when flying was still in its infancy, and a passing aeroplane would attract a large audience.

The parish church of St Mary the Virgin is seen in the foreground, with the eastern end of Hallgate running around the perimeter of the churchyard. Cottingham Board School (and its playground), built in 1892 after the 1870 Education Act, and which later became Hallgate Junior School, dominates the top half of the photograph. St Mary's rectory (built in around 1847) with its large gardens is seen at the bottom left of the picture.

By contrast this aerial photograph taken in 2005 from a light aircraft shows the extent of the north-eastern end of Cottingham. St Mary's church is visible in the centre, as are the range of buildings that make up Hallgate School, with the school's playing fields the predominant green space. St Mary's rectory has been replaced by the Hallgarth Residential Care Home for the Elderly.

Several large developments of houses have been built on land that was undeveloped at the time of the first photograph.

Hall Gate, Cottingham

*C*ottingham's principal street runs from St Mary's church in the east towards the Manor House site in the west, and was known as Hallgate from at least the early fifteenth century. Hallgate literally means 'the hall street'.

This 1930s photograph shows the junction of Hallgate with King Street. Two busy shopping streets intersect and traffic lights were needed to control traffic at the junction, even though in comparison with the modern view traffic appears almost non-existent.

On the south side of the street is William Cussons Limited, a branch of the Hull grocers, where it was possible to buy all manner of provisions including a range of their own brand goods. Between the wars the corner became known locally as 'Cusson's Corner', named after the shop. The building has housed John Ford's gentlemen's outfitters since the 1980s.

Opposite Cussons, on the south-east corner of King Street and Hallgate is a bank. From around 1904 it was the premises of Richard Marshall's hairdressers and tobacconists. In 1913 Marshall's business moved and the building became home to the Cottingham branch of the Midland Bank; it is now the HSBC.

This street was and still is Cottingham's main shopping street, although it appears considerably busier in the modern photograph than in comparison to the view of 1910, with cars parked along the south side of the street.

In 1908 the Cottingham joiner and contractor John Henry Wright built a shop on the north side of Hallgate, seen here with the projecting second-floor bay window, veranda, and flagpole, to the designs of Alfred Lawrence. The shop was built for Charles J. Mudd, the grocer, on the site of Wright's yard. The Wrights lived in the flat above the shop.

At the same time John Wright altered the adjoining double-fronted Georgian house known as Ivy Leigh. A double shop front was added and it became a new post office for the Tadmans, and a branch of the London Joint Stock Bank.

Both buildings still house shops; Mudd's grocers have been replaced by Cooplands' bakers, and the post office and bank by a picture framers and travel agents.

Climb the steep, narrow spiral stone steps of St Mary's church tower and this is the view from the top.

This photograph, from around 1905, looks along the length of Hallgate towards the west end of the village. On the right-hand side of the picture, and hidden amongst trees, is the rectory for St Mary's church and its grounds.

On the left side of Hallgate a row of buildings houses shops; including Cottingham's first post office, run by the Tadman family, Frank Hatfield's pork butchers and William Knagg's barbers, amongst others.

At the top of the picture is the Hallgate Wesleyan Methodist Chapel built in 1876-7, and directly below that is a range of buildings belonging to the Thurloe family. These include the King William IV public house with its attached brewery (the brewery chimney can be clearly seen), maltings and grain warehouse.

The photograph taken in 2006 shows a very similar scene, with the road layout still recognisable, although Hallgate is now congested with traffic; the Wesleyan Chapel still dominates the picture, as does the King William IV, but the maltings were demolished in 1977 to make way for a supermarket and car park.

The northern end of King Street, from Hallgate to Northgate, was originally known as Broad Lane. The old name still survives in the name of the watercourse, Broad Lane Beck (now culverted) that runs under the road and under Hallgate School's playing fields. An unculverted section of beck remains and can be seen running alongside the boundary of Needler Hall.

The terraced houses and buildings seen on the west side of the street in this photograph from around 1904 have been demolished to make way for a block of purpose-built modern shops housing a chemist, tanning salon and gift shop. Beyond is the entrance to a car park belonging to East Riding Council.

Further north, the terrace of six houses, including a shop, known as 'Alice Ann's Buildings' survives. They were built around 1879 for Richard Teale, and named after his daughter. Beyond stands the Primitive Methodist Chapel, whose gable can be seen in the distance above the roofline of the houses. The chapel was built in 1861-2 for a congregation of 350 worshippers. The chapel closed in the 1930s and was extensively altered. Today it houses Modus, an interior design and soft furnishings shop.

*O*n the west side of King Street is The Duke of Cumberland, seen in this 1950s photograph, and owned at that time by the Hull Brewery Co. Ltd. Beyond, in the single-storey building, is a branch of Zerny's dry cleaners.

The next building along in this photograph houses a branch of the National Provincial Bank, but until around 1914 it was the Angel Inn. The Angel is listed in trade directories from around 1820. By 1840 beer was being brewed on the premises, and in December 1841 a bill of sale read: 'For Sale, Angel Inn, brewing utensils, 56 casks, 150 gallons of ale, dram shop, fixtures, etc.' When the Angel closed the Cottingham Memorial Club was housed in the building, until its move to Elmtree House (*c.* 1949).

Between the site of the Angel and the Tiger Inn (a Moors' and Robson's house) were Clifford's Newsagents and Northern Dairies. The Duke of Cumberland still dominates the modern picture. A newsagents and branch of Heron Frozen Foods occupy the shops up to the Tiger Inn.

*T*his photograph from around 1915 looks north from King Street, across its junction with Hallgate, and towards the northern section of King Street that was originally known as Broad Lane.

On the immediate left of the picture is the Tiger Inn, which was built in the mid-eighteenth century. The Tiger Inn was first listed in directories from 1820; by 1825 a brewhouse had been added to the rear. The victualler's name, Florence Gertrude Taylor, can be seen on the hanging signboard. She was licensee from 1914 until around 1930. Opposite, on the eastern side of King Street, are C. Jackson's Central Boot Stores, advertising all kinds of repairs neatly executed.

Interestingly, two chickens stroll along the pavement outside the Tiger Inn.

The junction is much busier now with traffic controlled by traffic lights. The Tiger Inn was extensively altered in 1923, to make the pub we see today. On the eastern side of King Street a branch of the HSBC has replaced Jackson's shop.

King Street. Cottingham.

52·21   NORTHGATE.   COTTINGHAM

*T*his was one of the village's principal streets, recorded as 'Northgate' as early as the fifteenth century, running parallel to Hallgate. By the eighteenth century Northgate had become part of the Cottingham-Hessle-Beverley turnpike, securing its importance and guaranteeing its maintenance.

This late 1920s photograph shows the western section of Northgate. The wall and part of Park House, which by this time was being

used as a private school, can be seen on the left of the picture. Opposite is the junction with George Street, and beyond twelve terraced houses built to the designs of architects Wheatley and Houldsworth by Hinch Brothers builders in 1925.

The modern photograph shows two terraces of fifteen houses built in around 1933 on the site of Park House. Beyond is the entrance to the King George V playing fields and the 1970s housing development of Queens Drive.

*I*n the foreground, on the north side of Northgate, is one of the village's pre-enclosure farmhouses, which survived long enough into the twentieth century to be recorded in this photograph from 1910. Beyond it is the detached Sarum House standing on the corner of Mill House Woods Lane. Sarum House was built in the late eighteenth century and was originally single-storeyed. It was raised to two storeys in 1908 by builder J.W. Wright for the owner Shelah Gray, and its stringcourse shows the pre-1908 roofline.

Further west along Northgate are two more typical single-storeyed East Yorkshire cottages, which is probably how Sarum House would have looked before its alteration. The land opposite, to the south of Hallgate, was developed between 1928 and 1938 for housing. Six semi-detached houses, Nos 19-33, were built by Cottingham builder Fred Whiting for himself and William Fewster. The farmhouse in the foreground was demolished to make way for the 1950s housing seen in the modern photograph.

NORTHGATE.
COTTINGHAM. H.J.T.

*T*he first Augustinian monastery, founded in 1322, by Thomas, the second Lord Wake, was situated in this part of Cottingham. Built of wood, it was a temporary structure and by 1324 the monks had relocated west, to the hamlet of Newton, to build Haltemprice Priory.

Northgate became a well-established route and in the fifteenth century was one of the village's three principal streets. By the eighteenth century the road was part of the Hull to Cottingham turnpike.

Several pre-enclosure farmhouses were situated along Northgate and these survived into the twentieth century. One of these can be seen here at the corner of Northgate and Millhouse Woods Lane. A range of farm buildings stand to the east of the farm house.

At the junction of Northgate and Linden Avenue is this terrace of four Edwardian houses (Nos 2-8), fronted in fashionable yellow brick. They were built by William Rudd in 1906, to the designs of architect E. Whitlock, for William

Sykes, who lived in Oakhurst, Dunswell Road. Beyond the terrace is a detached house, Priory Cottage, built in the 1880s.

The modern view shows the same terrace, albeit hidden by trees. Beyond Priory Cottage, named after the abandoned priory on the opposite of the road, modern housing has replaced the old farmhouse and its outbuildings.

*T*he 1901 census lists the Kirby, Robinson, Longfield, Cockerill, and Hayton families as resident in the row of five cottages on the eastern side of Beck Bank. The cottages, seen in this 1910 picture, overlooked the Mill Beck, which ran through the village from Mill Dam Springs in the north and supplied the Snuff Mill with water to power the milling equipment. The cottages survived until the 1950s when they were demolished to make way for the new Railway Hotel and its car park.

The garden on the left belonged to Bridge House, on Newgate Street. The last occupant, Miss Fanny Foster, lived there until the house was demolished in 1935.

The beck has since been culverted and runs under the front gardens of the terraced houses on the west side of the road. These houses were designed by George Jackson, and built by Henry and Charles Jaram between 1933 and 1937. A pleasant green area, made up partly of the remains of Bridge House's back garden and partly the filled-in Mill Beck, still remains at the corner of Thwaite Street and Beck Bank.

Beck Bank. Cottingham.

C ottingham is criss-crossed with streams or becks, which are fed by the numerous fresh water springs in the area. Beck Bank gets its name from the Mill Beck that ran along the south side of the road, and has been so called since at least the early fourteenth century. The watercourse originates at the north of Cottingham and runs through the village, eventually draining into the River Hull north of Clough Road.

For many years all these becks were open, but as demand for land for housing grew many of these watercourses were culverted or filled in, the water being diverted underground into the sewers. The beck that ran along Beck Bank is seen in this picture, which was taken around 1911. The beck was filled in and the ground levelled in the mid-twentieth century. Part of the grassed garden area at Beck Bank's junction with Newgate is the 'filled-in' Mill Beck.

When the Hull to Scarborough railway line opened in 1846 it crossed one of the village's main streets. Thwaite Street is a post-enclosure route, although the area known as Thwaite was first recorded in the early fourteenth century.

This photograph, taken around 1905, looks east along Thwaite Street. A gatekeeper at

Thwaite is recorded in the 1851 census, at which time the gates were worked manually. The crossing gates as they appear here date from 1885. By August 1906 a signal box had been erected and the gates were worked mechanically.

Beyond the crossing stands Beechdale Farm, occupied by cow-keeper George Train between around 1900 and 1930. Further east is a row of six single-storey cottages, the walls of which were painted with white lime wash, and the woodwork painted black. Their appearance earned them the name 'Domino Six' locally.

Thwaite Crossing now has 'drop down' barriers controlled remotely from Beverley. Beechdale Farm has been demolished, replaced by a block of flats called Beechdale Court. A 1970s housing development known as Beechdale was built on the farm's land.

Thwaite St. Cottingham.

*O*ver the railway crossing heading west on Thwaite Street was the site of one of Cottingham's pair of cannons, seen here on a postcard, *c.* 1918. The village acquired the two decommissioned 40-pounder guns in 1904 as decoration. The other one of the pair stood on West Green. This one on Thwaite Street was finally removed in 1934 when its woodwork rotted and became dangerous.

In the distance are Thwaite Street's two public houses, The Duke of York Inn and the Railway Hotel, and beyond that, amongst the trees, is Shardeloes, built in 1899 for the Tothill family by Alfred Gelder, and demolished in 2002-3.

On the south side of Thwaite Street now stand sixteen semi-detached houses, from the railway line to Snuff Mill Lane. They were built between 1935 and 1939 during the pre-war housing boom.

Most recently a block of flats has been built on the site of the old petrol station, which replaced the row of old cottages and shop next to The Duke of York Inn.

*A*ccording to the *Victoria County History for East Yorkshire*, Volume IV, Finkle Street existed as an offshoot of Hallgate in the early seventeenth century. In 1672 hearth tax returns show there were twenty households in Finkle Street, and the street would have appeared quite different from this photograph taken around 1908.

This picture shows the north side of Finkle Street looking eastwards towards the police station of 1878, and beyond a terrace of three houses (Nos 84-8) built in 1905 by William Whiting.

In the foreground are two early eighteenth-century houses. The occupants of the house furthest east have added a fashionable door-case and bow windows to what, in comparison with the unaltered house next door, appears to have been quite a modest cottage.

The 1901 census lists the families living in the street, most of whom were employed in manual work – market gardeners, wheelwrights, joiners, etc. The exceptions were John Beal and John Jackson, both policemen with the East Riding of Yorkshire Constabulary and stationed on Finkle Street.

Today the north side of Finkle Street is a mixture of old and modern housing that sit side by side surprisingly well.

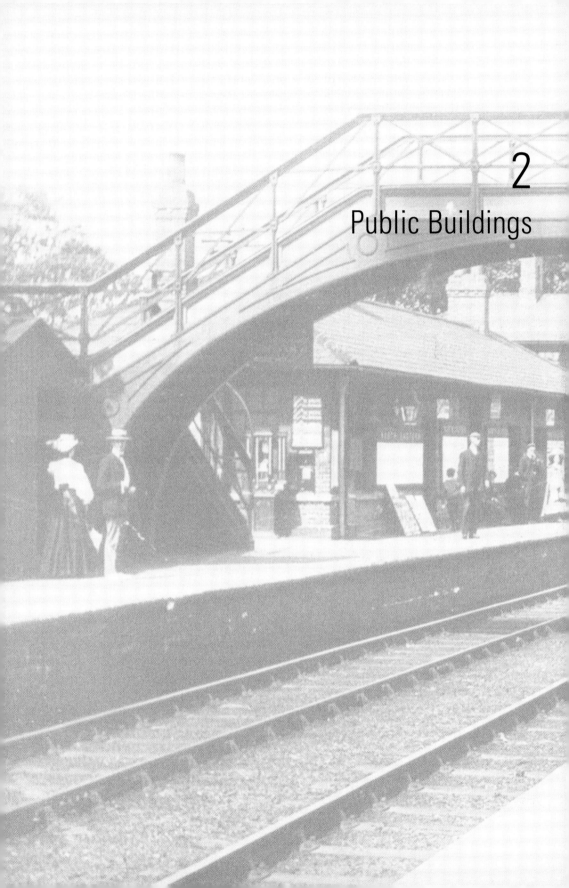

2
Public Buildings

Cottingham's first police station was built on the north side of Finkle Street. It was designed by Hull architects Smith and Broderick, and built in 1878, with six bays of round arched windows and arched doorway.

This image, from around 1904, records Finkle Street and the police station, with a group of local children enjoying the novelty of having their photograph taken. Opposite, on the south side of Finkle Street, are the grounds of Elmtree House, and to the south is a terrace of new houses, (Nos 107-17) built in 1903-4 by William Whiting.

In the years since this photograph was taken, the rest of the street has been developed. Houses (Nos 77-99) were built between 1906 and 1910 by father and son builders William and Harry Whiting.

The police station closed around 1970 and for many years was used by the Probation Service and Social Services. It has recently been sold, and is presently being converted into five luxury flats by a Hull developer. Today Finkle Street, like many other streets in the village, is congested with parked cars. No provision was made for parking when these houses were built.

*I*n 1844 the Hull and Selby Railway sought parliamentary approval to build a branch line along the thirty-one miles from Hull to Bridlington, passing through Cottingham. Permission was granted on 30 June 1845, and work started in 1846, with Messrs Jackson and Bean initially building a single track.

Cottingham's station was designed by York architect G.T. Andrews, and was built of local brick for the single-storey building with bay windows and arched chimney stacks. On the 6 October 1846 the line was opened by the 'Railway King', George Hudson. The convoy of engines and carriages arrived in Cottingham at 11.20 a.m., and was met by cheering crowds.

Improvements to the station were continual. By 1868 a stone east platform was constructed for passengers from New Village, and in 1902-3 the station was illuminated by gas. When this photograph was taken around 1908, Cottingham station was painted in the chocolate and cream livery of the North Eastern Railway. The station provided passengers with a waiting room, booking office, toilets, and storage for bicycles. The station staff tended flowerbeds, and won several prizes for best-kept station.

The station is quite different today. It appears neglected, is unmanned, and tickets have to be purchased on the train.

*T*his photograph from around 1910 shows Cottingham's station from the west, with the two-storey detached stationmaster's house to the north. The house was built in 1846, at the same time as the station, for the Hull and Selby Railway to the designs of the architect G.T. Andrews, and like the station it was built from brick and slate, with arched chimney stacks.

The census of 1851 lists William Phillips as the stationmaster, with a staff of one porter, two gatekeepers and three railway labourers. By 1901 three families were listed as living in the station yard: Robert Smith, the stationmaster, who lived in the Station House with his wife and children; John Burton, signalman, his wife and seven children; and David Green, another signalman, living with his wife, two children and a boarder.

One stationmaster, Robert Smith, was a keen gardener, and responsible for the station's prizes for best-kept station. He retired in 1910. The last stationmaster to live in the Station House was Francis J. Watson, who died in 1972, and soon afterwards the Station House was sold off. It is now a private house.

THE STATION
COTTINGHAM

Hallgate. Cottingham.

No. 8

The terrace of houses on the left was built around 1895 and known as Arlington Villas. No. 33 Hallgate (the house marked with a 'cross') was at the time of this photograph being used as a private school.

The school was listed in Kelly's directory for 1915 (the year this photograph was taken) and described as 'Athol House Private School'; its proprietress was Miss Margaret Gale. Athol House was one of several small private schools operating in Cottingham at the time, another being Eastholme College, which was almost directly opposite at Nos 22 and 24 Hallgate. Both schools ran concurrently, with some pupils attending Athol House as infants before progressing to the larger school across the road.

Today, No. 33 Hallgate has been returned to use as a private house. The two semi-detached houses, seen here on the left, were built along with six other pairs between 1933 and 1936 in the space between the corner of Beck Bank and Arlington Villas. A sign warning motorists of a school ahead refers to Hallgate Infants and Junior Schools, seen in the distance.

*E*astholme College (Nos 22 and 24 Hallgate), seen in these photographs of around 1905, was one of several private schools run in Cottingham during the early years of the twentieth century. Eastholme, listed in trade directories from the 1880s, was run by unmarried sisters Lucy and Annie Elizabeth Lister. The school catered for boarders as well as day pupils, and educated both boys and girls. In 1901 there were ten girls boarding at the school on the night of the census.

At its height up to thirty pupils were being educated there, with several teachers employed. The school trained its own pupil-teachers, who taught the juniors, and eventually became fully qualified teachers themselves. As Eastholme was no longer mentioned in trade directories

from the early 1920s, this may be when it closed. By this time it had been open for forty years, and the Lister sisters must have been at least sixty years of age.

The second picture shows the rear of Eastholme College, with teachers, pupils and domestic staff gathered to be photographed. Latterly the pupils wore uniforms, the girls with blue skirts and jackets, white blouses and white hats with blue ribbons. The boys wore blue suits and white shirts.

The present-day photograph shows Nos 22 and 24 as separate residential houses, both showing the tell-tale features of modernisation. No. 22 has replaced a window with garage doors; cars were not a consideration in the 1870s when these two houses were built.

*T*he area, known as High Cottingham, was enclosed in 1793. By 1800 the Hull banker Thomas Thompson had bought a fifty-four-acre plot of this land on which to build himself and his family a house.

Work began in 1805, with a shelter belt of trees being planted on the northern and eastern sides of the estate. The foundation stone of Cottingham Castle was laid in 1808 and by June 1816 the house was finished. Cottingham Castle had quite a chequered history. Thomas Thompson died in Paris in 1828, leaving the house to his son, Major-General Thomas Perronet Thompson, who chose not to live there. The house was eventually rented to J.B. Barkworth but was destroyed by fire in May 1861.

One of the surviving features of the house and estate was the gateway, through which a driveway led up to the house. The gateway is pictured here around 1909. The castle gates remained in use as the entrance to the sanatorium that was built on the site. In the 1960s, the narrow stone gateway was thought to be causing an obstruction to ambulances and other traffic entering the hospital and was demolished. The site of the gateway is still used as an entrance to Castle Hill Hospital, entrance No. 3, giving access to the medical wards and academic cardiology department.

Castle Hill Sanatorium, Cottingham, Yorkshire.   15824

*I*n 1913 Hull Corporation bought the derelict site of Thomas Thompson's Cottingham Castle with the intention of building a new sanatorium. The Hull Sanatorium was built between 1913 and 1916 to the designs of Joseph H. Hurst. It was intended as a replacement for the old infectious diseases hospital on Hedon Road, which had served the city since 1885.

The new Hull Sanatorium opened on 29 June 1916, made up of single-storey wards, well spaced-out across the site to reduce the risk of cross infection. Many were 'open air' wards with verandas, designed to allow the patients suffering from pulmonary tuberculosis access to fresh air, day and night. The large three-storey building seen at the centre of this 1920s photograph was used as nurses' accommodation.

Over the last twenty years Castle Hill Hospital, as it is now known, has changed beyond recognition. Old wards have been demolished and the site developed into a large, busy hospital, part of the Hull and East Yorkshire Hospitals NHS Trust. One survivor is the former nurses' accommodation block which now houses the supplies and finance departments.

When Thomas Thompson built his grand 'castellated' house and developed landscaped gardens on rising land to the west of Cottingham, he added a 'folly', seen in this picture of 1902. A folly was the fashionable garden feature of the day.

Thompson's folly was built in 1825 and took the form of a two-storey octagonal battlemented tower with gothic-style windows. Known as the 'prospect tower', it was built on the estate's highest point next to the road that ran from Beverley to Hessle. The tower was reputed to have a table at the top on which there was a map identifying all the places that could be seen.

Over the years the tower fell into a neglected state, and became overgrown and unsafe, and for the last few years it has been shrouded in scaffolding. Recently the folly has been given a new lease of life, weathered stonework has been replaced and the whole structure re-pointed. In 2006 the scaffolding was removed and Thompson's folly can now be seen restored to its former glory standing amongst the mature woodland in the grounds of Castle Hill Hospital.

Look-out Tower Cottingham castle

A natural fresh water supply known as Keldgate Springs rises up from the chalk on Eppleworth Road. Bore holes were sunk in the area and by 1908 a reinforced concrete reservoir with a 10-million-gallon capacity had been built on Keldgate Road, off Harland Way, to store water. In 1935 a second reservoir was built, again of reinforced concrete, with a capacity of 8 million gallons.

The second reservoir is pictured here in this photograph from the late 1930s; on the front it bears a date stone of 1935, and the three crowns coat of arms of the City of Hull. It was built into the hillside on rising land to the north-west, above the village towards Skidby, for the Hull Waterworks Co.

In the 1970s a new pumping station, storage reservoirs and bore holes were built at Keldgate to increase capacity. Today the Keldgate site is maintained by Yorkshire Water, who continue to invest in the site, which provides drinking water for Hull, Skidby and parts of Cottingham and Beverley.

*F*or many years Catholics in Cottingham worshipped in a large conservatory at Cherry Garth on Beck Bank, the home of the Hildyard family, but as the congregation numbers increased the need arose to find a suitable site to build a church.

Members of the congregation financed the purchase of a plot of land on the west side of Carrington Avenue, off Newgate Street, with Father Alphonsus Wannyn organising the planning and construction of the building. The modestly designed church, built out of plain rendered brick, was finished in 1929, and Bishop Shine consecrated the church of the Holy Cross on the 7 April that year. A detached priest's house (at No. 3 Carrington

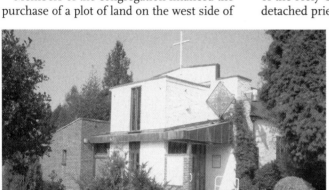

Avenue, next to the church) was added in 1939, designed by Arthur Windross and Partners and built by David Smith. This photograph, taken in 1941, shows the church as it was built.

When more accommodation was needed in the 1980s, the building was expanded sideways and the whole orientation of worship changed into a semi-circle around a central altar. In 1999 the church was badly damaged in an arson attack, but was soon restored, and open again for worship.

Zion Chapel Cottingham M.AR 4

Cottingham has a long history of Nonconformist worship, with John Wesley visiting Cottingham to preach on several occasions. The Zion Congregational church was built in 1819 on the southern side of Hallgate. The Zion Manse was added between 1852 and 1865 as a residence for the incumbent minister. The church is pictured here in 1908.

In 1967 a preservation order was placed on the church and it was described as a fine example of Georgian church building. However, a shortage of ministers in the 1970s led the Newland and Cottingham Zion congregations to join and become one church worshipping in two centres. The current combined church membership is around 100.

The building remains little changed today.

In 1992 two attractive windows of blue glass were installed to celebrate 300 years of independent worship on the site. The Manse became expensive to maintain and was sold off in the 1990s; it is now a private house. The garden at the front of the church now provides car parking for church users.

*T*he oldest building in Cottingham is the parish church dedicated to the Blessed Virgin Mary. The church is cruciform with a central tower. The nave, built in the decorated style of English Gothic architecture, and the chancel, in Perpendicular style, date from the fourteenth century. Pinnacles were added to the tower around 1744, and the clock replaced around 1875.

This photograph from 1906 shows St Mary's church looking east from Hallgate. The eastern part of Hallgate, around the churchyard's perimeter, was known as Kirkgate by around 1338.

On the north side of Hallgate, St Mary's rectory stands amongst trees, behind the wall and railings, and in the distance is Cottingham's Board School, built in 1892-3. Perhaps this is where the boys in the photograph have come from, for the clock on St Mary's tower reads 4.30 p.m., and school would have finished for the day.

The modern view remains remarkably unchanged. The board school has become Hallgate Junior School. The rectory has been demolished, making way for Hallgate Infants School and Hallgarth Residential Home for the Elderly.

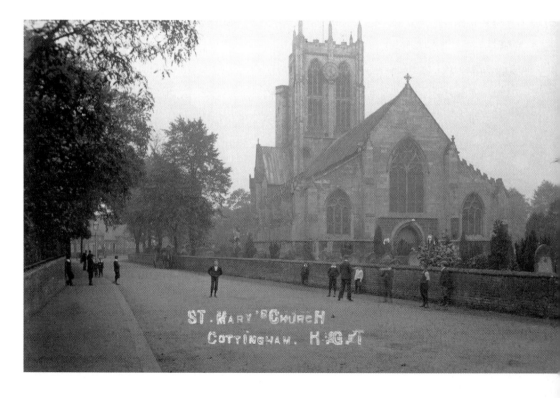

3

Trade and Industry

This public house was built between 1799 and 1801 for Robert Johnson, and was originally known as 'The Prince of Wales'. When the Prince ascended the throne in 1830, the pub's name was changed to reflect the event, although it was 1834 before the trade directories adopted the name change.

At the rear of the pub is a large range of outbuildings including a coach house and stables. In the 1880s the then-landlord, William Thurloe, added a brewery to the rear of the pub. Next to the pub, on the far left of this 1920s photograph, are the maltings where barley was malted as part of the brewing process.

The King William IV pub, brewery and maltings stayed in the Thurloe family until they were sold to the Hull Brewery Co. Ltd in 1893, at which time brewing ceased. Today the 'King Billy', as it's known locally, is little changed on the outside. The brew house behind has been incorporated into the pub as a function room known as the 'Old Brewery'. The maltings were demolished in 1977 to make way for a public car park.

*O*pposite Northgate's junction with King Street stands the Cross Keys public house. The Cross Keys was built in the early nineteenth century, and is listed as a pub in trade directories from that date. The 1901 census and Kelly's 1905 directory lists Mary Elizabeth Cockerline as the victualler, a widow living there with her three grown-up children. This photograph shows William Jacklin as the licensee, and dates it to around 1908.

Beyond the pub, in the terrace of houses, is an archway leading through cottages called Providence Place, but known locally as 'Sweeps Square'. Further east is a house with a shop front (built *c.* 1869) which traded as a grocer's and beer off-licence.

The Cross Keys now stands on its own, the terrace of houses and Providence Place having been demolished to give access to the pub's car park to the rear. The pub front as it appears today dates from an alteration of around 1920, when the brickwork was rendered and larger windows were added. Beyond, the house and shop that stood empty for many years have recently found a new lease of life as a dental surgery.

*S*tanding at the north-east corner of the Market Green, The Duke of Cumberland is thought to be Cottingham's oldest public house and dates from the late seventeenth century. It displays typical building features from that date, with its distinctively shaped Dutch gables and brick stringcourse. These features can be clearly seen in this 1920s photograph of the building's southern elevation.

It was first recorded as The Duke of Cumberland's Head in 1775, when it changed hands. Trade directories from the 1820s record the pub as The Duke of Cumberland with Richard Farnhill as victualler.

In the 1850s the landlord, William Green, was linked with the brewery that stood in Broad Lane (the northern section of King Street). The 1851 census describes William as an innkeeper and brewer; this was probably the source of the inn's beer.

The Duke of Cumberland still retains its original exterior features, although the interior has changed vastly over the years. This Hull Brewery photograph of the 1960s records a rather cluttered lounge, quite different from today.

*S*tanding on the eastern side of West Green is The Blue Bell public house. Robert Stephenson built it as a large detached house in the early nineteenth century, and it was listed as a pub in trade directories from 1823 onwards. The Blue Bell was enlarged at the turn of the twentieth century and again in 1926.

The man standing in the pub's doorway in this 1920s photograph is possibly the son of the landlady, Agnes Ellen F. Mears, accompanied by his faithful dog. Agnes took over the licence of The Blue Bell when her husband Samuel died in around 1917 and held it until at least 1939.

Samuel had been licensee since approximately 1910, and was often listed as both a victualler and a pig breeder/dealer; it was not uncommon for licensees to have more than one occupation. Pigs were bred, raised and slaughtered in the single-storey agricultural building to the right of the pub.

The frontage of the pub has had mock-Tudor timber framing added, and internally has been expanded into the single-storey building adjoining the pub, which now houses the dining room.

THWAITE STREET COTTINGHAM.

*O*n the northern side of Thwaite Street stood two of Cottingham's public houses; The Duke of York Inn and the Railway Hotel.

The Duke of York Inn had been listed in trade directories since the early nineteenth century. The last landlord was Jonas Pickles, there from 1917 until the pub's closure sometime between 1919 and 1921. Compensation of £750 was awarded to Pickles and the building's owners at the Beverley Quarter Sessions in October 1919 for the loss of the licence.

Further west is the Railway Hotel. Originally known as the Bay Horse, (*c.* 1840), then the Tiger (*c.* 1850), the first mention of the Railway Tavern on Thwaite Street was in Kelly's 1872 directory. This photograph dates from around 1906, when Walter Linskill was licensee, and the pub advertised 'good stabling'.

A new Railway Hotel was planned in 1938, but it wasn't until the 1950s that building work commenced. The new pub was built further west, and the 'old' Railway continued trading until the new pub opened. The old pub was then demolished. The present Railway Hotel, its car park, and a block of new flats now fill the site of the two old pubs and row of cottages.

*T*owards the end of the Second World War, the council began to look at the provision of more social housing on the south side of Cottingham. In 1945 work started on the Southwood Estate, later known as the Bacon Garth Estate. Demand was such that in the 1960s work began to build even more local-authority housing to the south of the village on a new road called the Parkway.

It was at this time that the public house known as the Black Prince was built, as seen in this photograph from around 1969. And along with a parade of shops to its south, it became the hub of the community. The pub

was named after Edward of Woodstock, the son of Edward III, born in 1330. Lord of the Manor of Cottingham and Prince of Wales, Edward became known as the Black Prince because of the armour he wore going into battle. Edward died in 1376, aged forty-three.

In the 1990s, the Mansfield Brewery modernised the pub, and it reopened on 22 September 1997 with a new name, 'The Friar Tuck'. This proved to be unpopular with locals, and within six months it returned to being called the Black Prince.

W illiam Grant's grocers and tea dealers business was situated on the south-eastern junction of George Street and Crescent Street. The shop was built with the adjoining six terraced houses between 1901 and 1906 by Joseph Sangwin for Ernest and Charles Tipple.

William was listed in the 1901 census as a gardener, living on George Street with his wife Mary and six children. It wasn't until Kelly's trade directory of 1905 that he was described as a shopkeeper.

This photograph of William's shop dates from around 1907, and shows a typical shop front of that era, with jars of sweets, tins and bottles displayed in the window. Above the door, a sign reads, 'William Grant, licensed to sell tobacco.'

The children in the photo are possibly three of William's: Ethel (eight years old in 1901), Stanley (three months old in 1901) and another daughter, born after the 1901 census.

The modern photograph shows that the shop front has been replaced by a house window. Ironically, a sign on the corner of Crescent Street directs delivery lorries towards the local supermarket, the rise of which heralded the demise of corner shops like William Grant's.

*B*uilder William Whiting, his wife Mildred and their nine children arrived in Cottingham around 1900 from Wainfleet in Lincolnshire. William's first business premises were on George Street, and he is listed there in Kelly's directory for 1905.

In 1904 William submitted plans to build two semi-detached houses on Hallgate.

William built the houses himself, calling them Grosvenor Villas (Nos 199 and 201). The houses are seen in this photograph around 1906. The Whiting family lived at No. 201 and William ran his business from the large yard to the rear of the property.

Kelly's directory for 1915 lists William as a builder at No. 201 Hallgate, and his son Harry (also a builder) as living at Claremont Villas on Finkle Street. In August 1917 William was struck by lightning and killed, leaving his other son, Fred, to take over the business.

F.J Whiting became part of the Marsden building group in 1988, and they still operate from the yard at the rear of No. 201. Shop fronts have been added to the two houses at Nos 199 and 201. The name of Cottingham's most prolific builders lives on in Whiting Court, a development of new houses built off Finkle Street.

*L*ike most villages at the turn of the twentieth century, Cottingham was self-sufficient in the production of meats, and had several butchers.

Samuel Jones specialised in the slaughter and butchery of pigs for his butcher's shops, both in the village and in Hull's market hall. Samuel, of Welsh origin, first appeared in the trade directories for Cottingham in 1905. By 1929 he was described in Kelly's directory as a 'Pork Butcher and Pig Dealer', at No. 158 Finkle Street. The business continued as a family concern well into the 1950s, the site of which, on Finkle Street, has recently been redeveloped.

This picture dates from the 1920s, and shows the Jones' lorry (advertising his business) making either a delivery or collection somewhere in the Cottingham area.

The modern photograph shows one of the two remaining butcher's shops left in Cottingham. Both shop owners recently joined forces to remind village residents to 'use them – or lose them', something which would dramatically change shopping in the village.

Several builders were responsible for Cottingham's growth in the 1930s. One of these men was Percy Buckle.

Percy, the son of Jabez Buckle, a bricklayer, was born at the family home on Waterloo Street, Hull. He followed in his father's footsteps and in 1898 he became apprenticed to Benjamin Musgrave, builder, of Beverley Road, Hull. The apprenticeship lasted for five years, and Percy's weekly wage started at five shillings in year one, increasing to eleven shillings in year five. Once qualified, Percy worked as a builder in Hull, living with his own family on Alliance Avenue.

In the 1930s Percy acquired land on Hull Road to build houses, and it was from here that he ran his business. Stationery from that era shows his business address as 'Overlands, 35, Hull Road', seen here in 1937 and in the modern photograph.

In the years 1933-39 Buckle's built houses all over the village, including Outlands Road, Dene Road, West End Road, and Overland Road. The houses he built were mostly designed by architect Jesse Taylor, and have a very distinctive style. Buckle's houses can still be seen in Cottingham, providing well-built, spacious family accommodation.

*T*he building on the left, seen here around 1909, was built in the early nineteenth century, and housed two shops: Frank Hatfield's pork butchers and Cottingham's first post office, run by the Tadmans.

Hatfield's butchers expanded into the adjoining shop in 1910, when the post office moved, and continued in business until the 1970s. Herbert Geoffrey Tadman was first listed at the post office in trade directories from 1899. By 1906 Herbert was described in directories as stationer, coal merchant, tea dealer, postmaster and registrar of births and deaths. Herbert's younger brother Harold took over the running of the post office from 1909, and moved the business further west along Hallgate in 1910.

Next to the post office is the gable end of a barn, which is reputed to have been the first registered meeting place for the Primitive Methodist congregation in Cottingham; by 1914, the barn and the white house next to it had been demolished and replaced with two purpose-built shops for Messrs Pybus and Tutill.

Paley and Donkin's carpet shop moved into the premises of Hatfield's butchers in the 1970s and is still there today. A Chinese restaurant and a branch of the Lloyds TSB occupy the adjoining shops.

*I*n 1893, John Paley and Robert Donkin started making press cloth at the Snuff Mill for the oil-seed crushing industry. The business expanded and they moved into new premises at Station Mills, off Northgate, in 1904. By 1914 the factory was one of Cottingham's largest employers, with sixty girls and twelve men working there.

Paley and Donkin also played an important part in the village's social life. In October 1913 Robert Donkin opened a cinema with seats for 400. It was known as the Don Picture Palace, and was situated in an adapted factory building. The inside of the cinema is shown in this photograph in around 1913. The films shown were silent, with piano or gramophone as accompaniment.

This aerial photograph of the factory site from the late 1930s shows a detached house in the centre, built around 1935 to the designs of Blackmore and Sykes, and occupied by the founder's family.

The factory diversified in the 1950s when Paley and Donkin started to produce carpets. The mill finally closed in 1981, and today Station Mills houses a garage and number of small industrial units.

Arthur Brocklesby started his business by opening a greengrocers-cum-general store in a yard off Northgate in 1911, the site of which is now the entrance to the car park of the Cross Keys public house.

By 1914 the business had expanded and Arthur opened a shop at No. 129 Hallgate, pictured here in this photograph of September 1933. A sign above the door advertises that the shop is licensed to deal in game, with rabbits and hares hanging outside ready for the pot. The windows display an amazing range of fresh fruit and vegetables, hams, and tinned and bottled produce to tempt the customer in.

Brocklesby's also had a second shop in the village, on Finkle Street.

For the last sixteen years, No. 129 Hallgate has been the premises of butcher Tim May, who moved in from the shop next door. Again a tempting selection of fresh meat is on display in the window, although modern hygiene rules prevent food being hung outside the shop. The other half of Brocklesby's shop is now a delicatessen and sandwich shop run by Ritchie, Tim May's son.

On the left-hand side of the picture is the shop of Cecil Herbert Beal. We are indebted to Mr Beal; he was one of Cottingham's postcard producers without whom this book would not have been possible.

Cecil Beal was born at Sledmere in 1888. His father was a police constable with the East Riding Constabulary, and moved to Cottingham sometime before 1901. When he first appears in trade directories in 1910, Cecil is listed as a hairdresser, but by 1914 he is listed as a newsagent too.

This picture from the early 1920s shows the location of his shop on the south side of Hallgate. Outside, newspaper hoardings show the day's headlines. Tobacco, stationery and hair cutting are advertised too, with a red and white striped barber's pole sticking out into the street. At the junction of Hallgate with King Street, a policeman directs what little traffic there is.

The site of Beal's shop was swallowed up when the bank on the corner of King Street expanded; it is now a branch of the HSBC. The road junction is much busier and now has traffic lights, which were first introduced in the 1930s.

There had been a mill to the north of Cottingham since medieval times. Originally it was a watermill fed by Mill Dam Springs and Mill Beck (which runs south through the village to also feed the South or Snuff Mill with water).

The windmill was of a typical East Riding design with four sails, similar in design to the mill at Skidby, and was built to operate the grindstones when the water in the Mill Beck was low.

After the water-pumping station opened in 1890 at Mill Dam the water table dropped significantly and the mill had to rely on wind power. The mill eventually ran on just two sails, as seen in this photo of around 1905. A steam engine was used for a time to power the mill just before its closure.

Bulmer's trade directory for 1893 lists the last miller as Isaac Needham, of Northgate Mill, but no further records can be found and the mill had been demolished by around 1910.

No trace of the mill exists now, and the watercourse has been culverted so that it runs underground. Mill Beck Lane (off Northgate) runs in roughly the same alignment.

OLD MILL.

4

Notable Buildings

Garden Hallgate House, Cottingham.

*I*n 1769 John Wray, the Hull merchant, bought land between Hallgate and Finkle Street. Hallgate House had been built by 1779, and was inhabited by John Wray junior after his father's death.

The house passed to Adrian Haworth in 1789, and to John Horsley in 1822. It was best known as the home of the Payne family, who lived there for many years.

It is rumoured that one of the house's owners bought the land opposite, now the Memorial Gardens, to prevent any future development spoiling their view!

The house was eventually vacated and turned into a Co-operative store in the 1950s. Most recently it has been divided into individual shop units, and now bears little resemblance to the once elegant dwelling.

The rear of the house and its gardens, which extended south towards Finkle Street, can be seen in these photographs from around 1910. These images are impossible to reproduce now as developments of modern housing have been built where the manicured lawns and greenhouses once stood.

At the turn of the twentieth century the rectory to St Mary's church stood in its own grounds at the north-eastern junction of Hallgate and Broad Lane (King Street). This house replaced an earlier one which the Revd Overton pronounced unsuitable for its purpose.

The rectory, seen in this photograph of 1907, was designed by architect William Richardson and built in 1847. The cost was £1,065, but the churchwardens' accounts from the time show that £155 was saved from the total amount by salvaging materials from the old house!

In 1901 the Revd Henry Ramsden, his wife, their two daughters and three servants were all living in the property on the night of the census. By the 1970s the rectory was becoming expensive to maintain, and in 1975 another new rectory was built on the site of Ivy House, with the portico and door-case being salvaged from the old rectory and incorporated into the new house.

The site of the old rectory and its gardens was sold to Humberside County Council, who built the Hallgarth Residential Home for the Elderly and Hallgate Infants School on the land.

The Rectory
Cottingham

*I*vy House stood in the western end of St Mary's churchyard amongst the gravestones. The house was built in the mid-1800s, and was thought to be home to the surgeon Samuel Watson in the 1870s. Bulmer's trade directory of 1892 lists Robert Garton as resident at Ivy House, with the address described simply as 'Churchyard'.

In the 1901 census Ivy House was inhabited by William Robinson, aged

sixty, his wife Rebecca, and their children Arthur, Edith and Eva. This picture from around 1903 shows the house covered with ivy, possibly the origin of its name, and as the home and business of W. Robinson, who was described as a gardener and florist. The house remained in the Robinson family until the 1970s, when William's last unmarried

daughter died. The house was finally demolished in 1974.

The new rectory for St Mary's church, built in 1975, stands on the site of Ivy House. It replaced the old rectory across the road on the northern side of Hallgate, which was in need of extensive, uneconomical repairs, and eventually demolished.

Situated on the north side of Northgate, Park House was built for Alice Clegg, the widow of Benjamin Clegg. By 1848 the house had passed to Thomas Wilson, the Hull merchant and founder of the shipping line. Thomas was responsible for extending and modernising the house, and this photograph from around 1912 shows the two phases of the building.

On 21 June 1869, Thomas died at Park House, and by the 1890s the house had passed to his son, David Wilson JP. The 1901 census lists the widow Elizabeth Sanderson as resident, along with two visitors. Also living-in on the night of the census were a cook, a kitchen maid, a butler, and four general domestic maids.

Park House eventually became a private school before finally being demolished in the 1930s. It was replaced by two terraces of fifteen houses (Nos 206-234), built around 1933 for Francis Plummer. The King George V playing field was laid out on land that had been Park House's gardens.

*S*hardeloes, on the north side of Newgate Street, was one of many large private houses built in the village by Hull's wealthy families. It was designed by William Alfred Gelder, and built in 1889 for Waring William Tothill. The house was enlarged for the Tothill family in 1903. This photograph of the house in 1905 shows part of the 1903 alterations, a single-storey extension, which housed a billiard room.

The house then passed briefly into the ownership of Ernest Ingleby, a stock and share broker, before being occupied by Captain Ambrose Good JP. Captain Good was a director of the Hull shipping merchants John Good and Sons Ltd, a member of the Zion Congregational Church and chairman of the Cottingham branch of the British Legion.

Shardeloes was eventually demolished in 2002-3, in spite of vociferous local opposition, and has been replaced by a large block of retirement flats built by McCarthy and Stone, offering secure warden-controlled accommodation for the over fifty-fives.

Joseph Milburn, described as a 'Gentleman of Cottingham', bought land on the north side of South Street in 1786. By 1800, Joseph had this elegant, two-storeyed, three-bay house built on the land. It was constructed from local brick and slate.

When Joseph died in 1810, the house passed to his widow Mary, who lived there until her death in 1824. The house was then owned by the Warner family until the late 1840s. The 1851 census records Elizabeth and Mary Travis as resident with three servants.

Trade directories from 1890 onwards list William Dunkirk Richardson and his family as living at South Street House, and they were still living there in 1901 when the census was

taken. William, aged eighty-one, was described as living on his own means. His wife Elizabeth (aged seventy-eight), their grandson Frederick (aged eleven), and one domestic servant were also resident in the house. The Richardson family were listed in trade directories at the house until 1915, and would have been in residence when this photograph of around 1904 was taken.

The modern photograph shows that South Street House is still used as a private dwelling.

*C*herry Garth was originally known as Beck Bank House when it was built in the early 1700s. In 1866 the owner, Dyas Lofthouse, had the house rebuilt with Dutch-style gables, and it can be seen on the eastern side of Beck Bank in this photograph, *c*. 1910.

The next owner was Walter Owbridge, the Hull lung-tonic manufacturer. The Owbridge family were in residence in 1901, and the census lists Walter (aged fifty-seven), his wife Emma (aged thirty-three) and their three children. Also listed were six domestic servants.

The Hildyards were the last family to inhabit the house, and lived there from the 1920s until the start of the Second World War. It was at this time that the large glass conservatory was used as a meeting place for Cottingham's Roman Catholics.

The house was converted into flats before finally being demolished in 1984. It has been replaced with purpose-built flats that retain the name 'Cherry Garth'. The stream in the old photograph is unculverted: now filled in, it forms the front gardens of the houses on the west side of Beck Bank.

This is possibly the only surviving pre-enclosure farmhouse in the village centre. It stands on the southern side of Northgate, opposite the entrance to Park Lane.

The house, which was probably known as 'Northolme' at the turn of the twentieth century, was built in the early eighteenth century for Robert Wilson, who lived there from 1729 until 1777. It then passed into the ownership of the Everingham family, before being sold in 1831 to the Hull tailor and draper Joseph Summers.

The fashionable Regency-style rendered frontage hides the true age of the house, but the wing projecting south to the rear of the house is built from long, thin bricks and pantiles, typical of vernacular buildings dating from the early 1700s.

The 1901 census lists the Jessop family resident at Northolme. It then passed to John Joseph Shuttleworth-Swaby, who ran a high-class boy's school, known as Latimer College, from the house. The school is listed in Kelly's directory for 1915.

The house's frontage is little changed since the 1922 photograph, but the railings and door-case have been replaced and the gate pillars to the right have been widened to allow cars access to a block of modern garages at the rear of the property.

Hallgate, Cottingham

*A*t the junction of Hallgate and Beck Bank stood Beckbridge Farm, seen in this photograph in around 1942, on the north side of Hallgate. Opposite is a row of semi-detached houses which were built in 1933-36 by Joseph Vickerman, to the plans of architect H. Roper Spencer, for Fred Owbridge. In the distance are Arlington Villas, a row of large terraced houses built around 1895, and beyond is St Mary's church tower.

Beckbridge Farm was home to Henry Lawson and his family, who were listed in directories from 1892 onwards. Henry was described as a 'farmer and cow-keeper'. The 1901 census lists Henry (aged forty-seven), his wife Fanny and their children – one daughter aged twenty-one, and five sons aged from nineteen to eight – all living in the house. The Lawson family moved to a farm at Skidby around 1912, after Henry's death.

By 1915 the property had been acquired by Tom Fussey, described as a cab proprietor in Kelly's directory, who ran a garage and bus service from that address. The area is still known locally as 'Fussey's Corner'.

The house was demolished in the 1960s, and in 1985 a development of modern houses known as Victoria's Way, which is pictured in the modern photograph, was built.

The four three-storeyed terraced houses, seen on the left of this 1905 photograph of Hallgate, were built on land next to a grain warehouse. The houses were built in the 1870s for William Thurloe, and had small front gardens surrounded by railings that projected onto the street.

William was not only the publican of the King William IV, but was listed in trade directories of the time as a brewer, maltster, and cab proprietor. The 1891 census lists William's three unmarried daughters, Anne, Hannah and Mary, living in one of his four houses. They were recorded as being supported by their own means, reflecting the success of their father's business. The house was still inhabited by a family member in 1901 when the census records William's granddaughter Lillian Thurloe (aged fourteen) living there with her mother (William's widowed daughter-in-law) and her stepfather John Featherstone.

The four terraced houses have all now had shop fronts added, and include an optician, dispensing chemist, fish and chip and lingerie shops. The railings and front gardens have long since gone to make way for the widening of Hallgate.

*H*idden behind a large brick wall on the south side of Thwaite Street is a house that used to form part of Cleminson Hall, one of Hull University's halls of residence.

The Bungalow was built around 1896 to the designs of architects Smith, Broderick and Lowther for the ship owner Charles Henry Wilson (later Lord Nunburnholme) who lived there until his move to Warter Priory. This photograph, which dates from around 1904, shows the house as it was originally built.

By 1915 the house had passed to Philip Hodgson, and afterwards to the Powell family. Samuel Powell had the Bungalow altered in 1926 by builders G. Houlton & Sons.

The university bought the Bungalow in 1951, and it became a hall of residence for students. More sleeping accommodation was built in 1962 and 1965, and until recently it was home to many university students. It now stands empty. The site has recently been advertised for sale to developers, with outline planning permission to demolish the 1960s blocks and build private housing. There are no plans to demolish the Bungalow.

*I*n 1945 the University College of Hull acquired the Lawns site on the north side of Northgate and Harland Way, complete with the army huts that had previously housed the American armed forces stationed there during the Second World War. It was initially known as Camp Hall and accommodated male students from the university.

The University began to redevelop the Lawns site in 1956-7 with the building of Ferens Hall. It was designed by architects Gillespie, Kidd and Coia in the Neo-Georgian style and provided purpose-built accommodation for the students. This photograph, which dates from around 1961, shows the extent of the hall.

Development continued on the Lawns site in 1963 when six purpose-built blocks of student accommodation were built, providing self-contained rooms, dining and meeting halls, and communal areas for up to 800 students. Ferens Hall and the Lawns Halls are still Hull University's main residences in Cottingham, providing accommodation for around 1,100 students.

*T*he Russian merchant John Hentig built Thwaite House in 1803 as a family home. After Hentig's death in 1853, David Wilson JP acquired the house, before selling it to his brother Charles Wilson. It was at this time that Thwaite House was extensively enlarged and re-fronted. During this period the gardens were landscaped by Hull gardener and botanist James Niven; he added a lake, and many rare and exotic species of plants.

By 1893 the house was in the ownership of Colonel William Edward Goddard JP. The Goddard family were part of Cottingham's busy social circle, holding many lavish parties at Thwaite House, and employing up to sixteen staff to cater for these gatherings.

On 3 March 1928, the University College of Hull purchased Thwaite House for £8,300 from Colonel Goddard's widow. Again the house was altered with several large extensions added to accommodate students. Thwaite House had now become Thwaite Hall, a hall of residence for students, and is recorded in this 1950s photograph.

Still home to many university students, the hall must boast the best grounds of all the student residences in Cottingham. The landscaped gardens of Thwaite House have been preserved and are now the university's botanic gardens.

The Hull tobacco merchant William Travis built this grand house in 1795, complete with fish pond and landscaped gardens. Travis owned the Snuff Mill and had originally built and lived in the mill house, but wanted a larger, grander, higher-status house.

Cottingham Hall was built on land belonging to the Snuff Mill, with a long driveway sweeping south from Thwaite Street. This view is of the rear of the house, and dates from around 1910.

It was occupied between the 1870s and early 1900s by the Hull ship-owner William Henry Heap Hutchinson, then in turn by Jeffrey Ringrose, Miss Reynolds and Neville H. Joy throughout the early twentieth century.

The house was demolished in 1935 to make way for housing developments, including Hall Walk and Mill Walk. In the 1960s the Hornbeam Drive housing development was built on land that had been part of Cottingham Hall's landscaped gardens.

5
Suburbs and Side Streets

*A*rlington Avenue runs south-west from Hallgate parallel to the southern boundary of St Mary's churchyard, with houses built along the street's southern side only. This photograph was taken around 1905.

The terraces of nineteen houses were built in two stages: Nos 1-10 were built in 1899, and Nos 11-19 were built in 1900. They were designed by architect James J. Adamson, and built by Joseph Sangwin for Sir James T. Woodhouse.

The houses were newly occupied when the 1901 census was taken and the occupations of the residents reflect the status of the new street. Almost all were white-collar workers or skilled craftsmen, including William Last (a watchmaker and jeweller), Charles Worte (the manager of the National Telephone Company), and William Whiting (a builder).

One of the street's residents was Robert Donkin, a founder of the press-cloth manufacturer Paley and

Donkin, who would go on to be one of the village's largest employers. Young Robert, aged twenty-six, lived with his mother and stepfather, and was described as an employer weaver on the census return.

Arlington Avenue is still a pleasant street overlooking the church. Many of the well-built Edwardian houses have retained their original features.

Baynard Avenue, Cottingham

S ervicemen returning from the First World War had such difficulty finding suitable accommodation that the government was forced to pass legislation enabling councils to build houses to rent. Cottingham Urban District Council was one of the councils that took advantage of this new law to build up its stock of affordable social housing for working-class families.

Land was purchased at the south-west of the village, and the lane originally known as Cross Shackett (linking South Street and West Green) was redeveloped as Baynard Avenue, named after the medieval castle site north of West Green. In 1921, Baynard Avenue and Southwood Road became the site of Cottingham's first council houses, which are seen here in this photograph of 1947. They were designed by Harry Andrew and built by Holliday and Barker.

Thirty-six houses were built in total, but sixty-six families applied to rent them, so selection criteria were drawn up to make the allocation fair. Highest priority was given to ex-servicemen with children, and lowest priority to civilians without children. The rents ranged from eleven to thirteen shillings per week depending on the size of the house. Several of the council houses on Baynard Avenue are now privately owned.

Carisbrook Avenue runs north from Newgate Street, and was not laid out until after the beginning of the twentieth century. The first houses were built closest to Newgate Street; on the west side of the street, Nos 1-7 were built in 1907-8 by George Lancaster, then Nos 2-12 were built on the east side in 1908-9, by Mark Crossland. The street developed in this manner, and by 1928 all the building land had been filled. The last house to be built was a detached bungalow, completed in 1929 by Fred Whiting for Ann E. Mudd, widow of Charles Mudd, the Hallgate grocer.

During the First World War, at the time of a national food shortage, land behind Carisbrook Avenue was used as allotments, and rented out to villagers at six shillings per year.

The present view of Carisbrook Avenue shows that little has changed in the street since the first photograph was taken around 1920, although the trees have matured, and like many other streets of this era built without provision for the motor car, it has cars parked along both sides most of the time.

Carisbrook Avenue. Cottingham. No. 21.

ENDYKE LANE   COTTINGHAM W.P.

*I*n 1819 Thomas Thompson, the Hull banker, persuaded the Overseers of the Poor in Cottingham to rent from the parish church an area of land of twelve acres. This land was bordered by Middledyke Lane, Inn Common Lane (now New Village Road) and Endyke Lane. It was divided into twenty smallholdings, to be let to families who had been receiving poor relief, on the condition that they made no further claim on the local parish.

The area became known as 'Paupers Gardens', but this was soon changed to the more respectable title of 'New Village'. By the 1840s many of the families living in New Village had built themselves homes, either self-funded or with money from charitable donations. These houses were simple, single-storey, brick and pan-tiled cottages that fronted onto Middledyke

and Endyke Lanes, as can be seen in this faded but rare photo from around 1914.

By 2001, only four of the original New Village cottages remained: most had been demolished to make way for larger modern houses. Only one of the original cottages now survives, at No. 20 Endyke Lane.

For many years Eppleworth Road was a main route west out of the village. It linked up with the Beverley to Hessle road that had been turnpiked in 1769. In 1774 the Eppleworth Road was turnpiked as far as the main Beverley road. Beyond, it continued through the hamlet of Eppleworth and joined the Kirkella to North Cave road. The name Eppleworth, the hamlet at the 'apple wood', was first recorded in the fourteenth century, although is probably much older and was part of the parish of Cottingham.

When this faded but rare photograph was taken at the turn of the twentieth century, Eppleworth Road was still a rural lane, with only a handful of houses built along its length. On the north side, Frederick Moulson built a terrace of four houses, set back from the road,

in 1883-4. Further west, in the new burial ground, a cemetery lodge and mausoleum chapel were built by Frank Witty in 1889 for Cottingham Local Government Board.

Almost all the houses on Eppleworth Road we see today date from the building boom of the 1920s and '30s when agricultural land on the western fringe of the village was bought up for house building.

*C*ottingham grew rapidly in size in the late nineteenth century and demand for housing resulted in the development of streets on what had previously been agricultural land at the eastern end of the village. One of these streets was Exeter Street, off New Village Road.

Exeter Street was first laid out in around 1904, and by 1909 was well established, as this picture shows. The new houses were popular with Cottingham's expanding 'white-collar' population with the street being situated so close to the station, making it easy for workers to commute into Hull.

At No. 2 Exeter Street was a grocery branch of the Hull Co-operative Society. It opened in 1906 and like many other corner shops served the housewives of the New Village Road area

well. The shop finally closed in 1967 after sixty-one years of service.

Exeter Street is still a popular residential street, although when the houses were built no provision was made for motor cars, so it has become fairly congested. A hair and beauty salon has replaced the Co-op.

George Street is named after George Knowsley, the owner of Cottingham Grange. He created the street, linking Northgate and Hallgate, after he bought land and closed an ancient right of way linking the two streets further west. In 1804, Knowsley sold off plots of land in an area known as 'Applegarths' on which the properties on and around George Street were built.

This photograph, taken in around 1905, shows George Street from the Hallgate end, looking towards Northgate. The four terraced houses on the east side of the street were built between 1855 and 1861 by George Gardner; the detached house beyond was built in 1867-8 by William Kirk. Further north is the yard of William Whiting, the builder; the street then dips into one of the village's lowest lying points.

This makes George Street prone to flooding when the Keldgate Springs (to the west of the village) flow. One such occasion was in the summer of 1912, when the street's junction with Crescent Street flooded after a heavy cloud-burst.

Modern George Street shows infill with early twentieth century and more modern housing, with the original terrace still occupied. The detached house is now the premises of solicitor Gwendoline Drewery.

GEORGE STREET.
COTTINGHAM.Hd.T.

W hen the Hull to Cottingham turnpike was opened in 1764 it ran along Hull Road, Inn Common Lane (now New Village Road), and ended at the western end of Northgate. By 1796 the turnpike had been extended to join the Beverley to Hessle turnpike west of the village. This road eventually became Harland Way as we know it today.

The land around was mostly agricultural, being part of the seventy-two acres of Harland Rise Farm. Further west, chalk was quarried in the nineteenth and early twentieth centuries to be used for building materials.

In 1888 the Local Board acquired land to be used as a burial ground between Harland Way and Eppleworth Road, previously the site of Low Mill.

The houses seen in this photograph of 1943, on the south side of Harland Way, were built by the Cottingham builder Fred Whiting between 1924 and 1927, overlooking farmland.

Those 1920s houses now overlook a modern development of new houses called The Woodlands, with Harland Way the route to and from secondary school for the majority of Cottingham's teenagers.

*B*efore the 1880s the Cottingham parish extended east to the River Hull. The parishes of Sutton and Cottingham were linked by a trackway that ran through the settlement of Newland and crossed the river at Stoneferry (roughly where the B & Q store is now).

In 1764 the Hull to Beverley turnpike was extended with a branch heading west towards Cottingham. The road ran through Newland along the old track from Sutton, with tolls collected at a toll-bar roughly where the Haworth Arms stands today. The turnpiked road was named Hull Road at its western end, and was for many years the main route to and from the village.

Being on the edge of the village, the fields either side of Hull Road were used to dump night soil and to dig clay to supply brickyards. The pre-war housing boom spread to Hull Road in 1938, and this photograph shows work about to start on nine houses by builder Percy Buckle.

These days Hull Road is a busy route to and from the village. Percy Buckle's houses have stood the test of time well, and the trees have matured, providing a cool leafy feel to the road.

'*I*gglemire', first recorded in the thirteenth century, was an area of low-lying marshy land at the eastern edge of Cottingham parish. By the eighteenth century a lane was recorded crossing the land, running west from the Beverley Road, to the north of Newland, and continuing into Cottingham. This became Igglemire or Inglemire Lane.

In the 1770s, an area of 513 acres of common meadow and pasture at Inglemire were enclosed, and by the end of the nineteenth century this farmland belonged to the Haworth family of Hull Bank House.

This photograph, taken in around 1905, shows Inglemire Lane as an undeveloped rural lane – at the turn of the twentieth century only a handful of houses had been built on it. At the Cottingham end, April Cottage (now No. 22) had been built in the 1840s for Charlotte Ellerton, and a detached house (now No. 13) had been built around 1871 for Henry Stephenson.

Inglemire Lane was heavily developed in the 1920s and '30s as demand for housing grew. On the street's north side, Nos 1-11 were built by Charles Kettlewell in 1928-9, and Nos 15-29 were built by George Needler in 1937-8. On the south side, houses Nos 2-20 were built by J.R. Cousins and William Garbutt in 1926-7, No. 28 by Fred Whiting around 1923, and Nos 30-32 (again by Whiting) around 1936. Today, Inglemire Lane is a busy thoroughfare, with its eastern end now part of Hull.

*T*his is one of the many pre-Second World War housing developments in Cottingham, built in a period when the village was expanding rapidly. The houses were bought by people from Hull who still worked in the city: with the opening of Priory Road, they could commute easily. Kingsway, seen in this photograph taken in around 1939, runs west from Priory Road, joining the Bacon Garth Estate via Link Road.

The first houses, at the junction with Priory Road, were built between 1936 and 1939. Twenty-four pairs of semi-detached houses, Nos 1-31, 33-57 and 16-54, were designed by architect Rowland D. Herbert and built by Cottingham builder Fred Whiting. Another three pairs of semi-detached houses, Nos 2-12, were designed by William Blanchard and built by Alan Taylor. Building work stopped as the Second World War started.

On the night of 25 February 1941, a bomb dropped by the Luftwaffe exploded in a field near No. 27 Priory Road causing damage to Nos 13, 24 and 57 Kingsway.

Modern Kingsway looks very similar, albeit with the addition of many more cars, although the houses were built with the provision of garages for motor cars.

KINGSWAY, COTTINGHAM .   No 21.

*A*long with several other streets in the north-eastern corner of the village, Linden Avenue was developed in the late nineteenth century. It runs parallel to the Hull to Scarborough railway line, which is on the far right beyond the trees.

In 1887 William Barnes built eight semi-detached houses, seen in this picture of around 1904, on the west side of the street. They were built for Charles Wake and numbered consecutively one to eight.

Before 1907 (when Cottingham Urban District Council accepted responsibility for the road's surface, lighting and drainage) Linden Avenue was a private road and as a result the road's surface appears to be little more than a muddy farm track.

The 1901 census records seven of the eight houses occupied and all the residents had 'white-collar' occupations. Listed at No. 8 was Arthur Moorby, headmaster of the board school on Hallgate: also resident were his wife Annie, their three children, a niece, and a servant.

By 1910 another fourteen semi-detached houses had been built further along the street, but it wasn't until 1939 that all the land was developed. Linden Avenue is still a popular residential street. The trees have now matured, screening the houses from the railway line.

*T*his street's first recorded name was Inn Common Lane after the 'inner' common, which lay to its north. The Cottingham Urban District Council officially changed the street's name sometime between 1905 and 1910 to New Village Road, (named after the settlement originally known as 'Paupers Gardens' but changed to the more respectable 'New Village').

This photograph shows the junction of New Village Road and Cornwall Street in around 1910. Cornwall, Devon and Exeter Streets were laid out just after the turn of the twentieth century.

The terrace of houses on the east side of Cornwall Street and the shop and adjoining terraced houses on New Village Road were all built in 1906-7 by George Maltby. The land had previously belonged to North View Farm, built around 1867 for George Padgett, whose land ran south towards Thwaite House. The 1901 census lists Henry Padgett (a market gardener), his wife Mary and their five children living there.

The corner shop was until recently Cottingham Cycles, but now stands empty. And the house next door, for many years a ladies hairdresser's, is now the office and showroom of Classical Gas.

COTTINGHAM. 1451810

*T*he middle section of the road that runs south through the village is Newgate Street (from Beck Bank to King Street), and is pictured here in around 1914. It was originally known as Newgate (new street) and first recorded in the sixteenth century.

On the south side of the street, beyond the trees, stood Cottingham House: originally the home of the Bacchus family, it was bought by Hull merchant James Milnes in 1744. The house later passed to several other prominent families; it was demolished in 1972.

Opposite, a terrace of Edwardian houses lines the north side of Newgate Street between Carisbrook and Carrington Avenues. Walter Garbutt built these houses, Nos 10-28, between 1907 and 1913.

The modern housing development off Longmans Lane was built on the site of the demolished Cottingham House. However, its lodge survives on the south side of Newgate Street. The Lodge was built around 1845 for Joseph Gee, the Hull merchant, who owned Cottingham House between the years 1841-60.

*A*s Cottingham expanded in the inter-war years, agricultural land on the outskirts of the village was sold off for house building. Land to the west of Hull Road belonging to the Mark Kirby Charity was sold in around 1932 to build Overland Road. The field, known locally as Paradise Close, had belonged to the charity since enclosure.

By 1934 the new road had been laid out, running south-west from Hull Road. The road itself was constructed of blocks of concrete, a very popular material first used in Cottingham in the 1930s by the Urban District Council, and requiring little or no maintenance.

Forty-eight semi-detached (and two detached) houses were built by Percy Buckle between 1934 and 1937, to be owned partly by Buckle and partly by the Mark Kirby Charity Trustees. This photograph, taken in 1936, shows the building work in progress.

In 1941 Overland Road was bombed by the Luftwaffe: on the night of the 15 February a bomb fell, trapping two women at No. 46, home of Ernest Charles Warnes and his family. On the night of the 17 February, four more bombs fell on the street, but did not explode.

Overland Road is still a residential street with generous family-sized houses.

Park Lane, Cottingham.

Raphael Tuck & Sons Ltd
London

*T*his lane was well established by the eighteenth century as a route to farms built on the former medieval deer park. The original road joined Northgate further west, but in 1804 the landowner, George Knowles, was allowed to re-route it around his land, to give the road the curving alignment we know today.

In the 1930s land to the north of Park Lane was sold off on behalf of the trustees of Cottingham Grange. This included 89 acres of Spring Park Farm, several market gardens and grassland.

Cottingham Urban District Council acquired land at the junction of Park Lane and Northgate with the intention of building 'social houses'. In 1933 eighteen new council houses, designed by Thomas Slack, were built on Park Lane, seen in this photograph of around 1938, and on Park Avenue. The houses were primarily intended for occupancy by agricultural workers.

Small estates of modern housing now fill the southern portion of Park Lane, but the area still retains its historical links with market gardens and agriculture.

long with Bricknell Avenue, Priory Road was laid out in around 1932 to link Cottingham with west Hull. The road was constructed of concrete sections, and was thought to need little maintenance. The new road was built along the alignment of the earlier Woods Lane, and is seen here in the 1950s.

Almost immediately, houses were built at both the Cottingham and Hull ends, with an estate of local authority housing, to be known as 'Priory Road Estate', planned for the middle section. This never came to fruition, leaving a green belt between the village and Hull.

The houses in the photograph were built in chronological order leaving the village, those

nearest (Nos 13-19 and 16-26) being built in 1932-3, and those further away (Nos 23-41 and 32-38) in 1937-9.

In the distance, amongst the trees, is Wood Lane Farm, better known locally as 'Fisher's Farm' after the Fisher family. The house and farm buildings date from 1839-55.

Priory Road is now a busy route to and from Cottingham. In 2006 Hull City Council gained permission to build a new cemetery on the open land outside the village, which will change the landscape forever.

SNUFF MILL LANE
COTTINGHAM

*S*nuff Mill Lane takes its name from the Snuff Mill that stood on the site of the village's old South Mill. It runs from Thwaite Street in the north, past the site of the Snuff Mill, and then out of the village in a south-easterly direction. The lane ran alongside the Mill Beck, seen in this photograph of 1907, which provided the mill with water to drive the milling machinery.

William Travis, a tobacco merchant and snuff manufacturer from Hull, bought the water mill in 1755 from William Long, and built the adjoining elegant Mill House around 1760. Travis eventually built Cottingham Hall in 1795 and moved there, renting out the Mill House.

Samuel Bolton worked the mill in 1823, making worsted cloth. It then passed to Paley and Donkin, who made press cloth there until 1904. The Mill was eventually demolished in the 1930s, but Snuff Mill House survived as a private house.

The beck was culverted in the 1960s and now runs under the grass verge at the north end of Snuff Mill Lane, before passing under the gardens of Snuff Mill House. The Hornbeam housing estate is built on land belonging to the Snuff Mill and Cottingham Hall.

*T*he road that runs south through the village has had several names. In the fifteenth century it was known as Newgate, with its western section being known as Southgate by 1793. It was during the early nineteenth century that this section of the road was first known as South Street.

This photograph from around 1914 shows the street as it was just after the turn of the century. The large Edwardian houses on the north side of South Street were built between 1907 and 1910, by the Cottingham builders William and Harry Whiting, to the designs of Alfred Lawrence.

On the south side of the street a large wall surrounds Elmfield House. A house has been on this site since around 1795, but the original had been replaced or rebuilt by around 1863. In 1901 Elmfield House was home to Henry Briggs, an eighty-five-year-old retired ship owner, his wife Mary, and their cook and housemaid.

South Street is now a busy thoroughfare, and choked with traffic most of the day. Elmfield House has lost its walled garden to make way for modern housing, and the house itself is in the process of being transformed into 'luxury' flats.

South Street, Cottingham

*O*riginally known as First Green Lane, St Margarets Avenue is now the site of more inter-war housing developments at the west of the village. It runs from Eppleworth Road in the north to the junction of Southwood and Castle Roads in the south.

At the road's north end, seen in this 1950s photograph, the houses and bungalows (Nos 1-45 and 2-48) all shared a common builder, John Crosskill, trading under the name of Kemp and Hall. Building began around 1934 and ended abruptly with the start of the Second World War.

By far the most interesting building on St Margarets Avenue is Bondyke House, at the south end. Designed by Hull architects Smith and Broderick and built for Thomas Bach, the house is built of red brick, tile-hung, with half-timbered gables. It was built around 1882, and is dated as such.

By 1893 the house was inhabited by William Merrikin, the Hull colour and paint manufacturer. The 1901 census lists him living there (aged seventy-six), along with his son and daughter, their housekeeper, cook and maid.

The modern view is little changed, although gardens have matured and, as in all streets, cars are now a prominent feature.

This photograph was taken in April 1937 to record the new houses that had been built on the west side of West End Road and the north side of Dene Road.

In the inter-war years Cottingham expanded all around the village's periphery and West End Road demonstrates this expansion at the west of the village, building on what, at the turn of the twentieth century, was little more than a country lane marking the village's west end and leading to the villages of Eppleworth and Skidby. The mature tree in front of the houses survives from an enclosure field boundary.

The fourteen semi-detached houses in the picture were designed by architect Jesse Taylor and built by local builder Percy Buckle between 1936 and 1938. Kelly's trade directory of 1939 lists several West End Road residents as 'private resident', signifying that the houses were occupied by white-collar workers.

These days, West End Road is still a residential area; trees in the houses' gardens have matured somewhat.

West End Road, Cottingham April 1937.

WEST GREEN COTTINGHAM.

W est Green, at the west end of the village, is thought to be much older than Market Green, and it's likely that the first market, licensed by King John, was held there. The first detailed map of Cottingham, dated 1839, shows houses grouped around West Green at the west end of Hallgate.

This photograph, from around 1905, shows a group of local children standing by the Boer War cannon, one of a pair that 'guarded' the easterly and westerly approaches to the village. The cannon remained on West Green until 1921, when it was seen as a source of danger to children and removed. Beyond the green is The Blue Bell Inn with a large board attached to the wall advertising the latest performance at the Grand Theatre in Hull.

The house adjoining The Blue Bell dates from around 1781, and the large semi-detached pair at the corner of Hallgate were built in 1873. West Green is no longer the most westerly point of the village, but The Blue Bell still overlooks a pleasant scene with mature trees, the first of which were planted between 1910 and 1914, and flowerbeds.

Other local titles published by The History Press

Haunted Hull

KEITH DADDY

Journey through the darker side of Hull, a city steeped in spooky tales that will captivate anyone with an interest in the supernatural history of the area. From creepy accounts from the city centre to phantoms of the theatre, haunted pubs and hospitals, the book contains a chilling range of ghostly phenomena. Drawing on historical and contemporary sources, you will read intriguing accounts of many ghostly goings-on in this haunted city.

978 07524 4018 7

Hull Pubs and Breweries

PAUL GIBSON

Hull city is renowned for its pubs and breweries. From back street taverns to historic hostelries, this fascinating selection of archive photographs records the drinking establishments that made the city famous. With anecdotes of landlords and regulars, celebration and sorrow, this book will appeal to readers who have visited public houses around Hull and, indeed, anyone with an interest in the history of the city.

978 07524 3284 7

Kingston upon Hull: The Second Selection

PAUL GIBSON

Kingston upon Hull is a city of great variety and contrast, including docks, industry, civic buildings and residential areas. This selection of archive images brings to life many of the streets and long-forgotten work places which have disappeared or have changed beyond recognition. This book offers many nostalgic memories for those who remember how the city used to be.

978 07524 2607 5

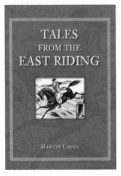

Tales from the East Riding

MARTIN LIMON

The old East Riding of Yorkshire has had a rich and varied past and Martin Limon's historical collection features some of the people, places and events that have made it that way. Here are tales of pygmies and giants, Roman villas and Victorian workhouses, famous industrialists and infamous highwaymen, all with a place in the county's history.

978 07524 4038 5

If you are interested in purchasing other books published by The History Press, or in case you have difficulty finding any of our books in your local bookshop, you can also place orders directly through our website

www.thehistorypress.co.uk